Thomas Mert

CHRISTIAN SPIRITUALITY SERIES

Brother Ramon SSF

Remember Me
Life's Changing Seasons
Praying the Bible
Praying the Jesus Prayer

Tony Castle

Evelyn Underhill on Prayer
The Prayers of Christina Rossetti
The Prayers of Lancelot Andrewes

Thomas Merton on Prayer

Compiled and edited

by

Tony Castle

Marshall Pickering

Marshall Morgan and Scott
Marshall Pickering
32 – 42 Cleveland Street
London W1P 5FB

First published in 1989 by Marshall Morgan and Scott Publications Ltd
Part of the Marshall Pickering Holdings Group

Acknowledgment is due to the Merton Legacy Trust for permission to use
extracts from Thomas Merton's works. These extracts appear in the sources
listed on page 29 of this book.

British Library CIP Data

Merton, Thomas, *1915 – 1968*
    Thomas Merton on prayer
    1. Christian life. Prayer
    I. Title II. Castle, Tony, *1938 –*
    III. Series
    248.3′2

    ISBN 0-551-01764-3

Text Set in Baskerville by Avocet Robinson
Printed in Great Britain by Henry Ling Ltd., at the Dorset Press,
Dorchester, Dorset

Contents

Introduction

A few weeks ago, in the Catholic High School for Girls, where I teach, we celebrated the Week of Prayer for Christian Unity with a special service. The Salvation Army Major who had been invited to give the address commenced with: 'How fortunate you Catholics are to have the wonderful writings of Thomas Merton.' He continued to expound at some depth! The girls were lost and afterwards asked, 'Who is Thomas Merton?'

It is understandable, but a tragedy, that most modern Roman Catholic young people have never heard of the American Trappist monk, who died over twenty years ago, just as most Anglican young people have never heard of Evelyn Underhill.

Merton was without doubt one of the most revolutionary thinkers and perceptive spiritual writers of modern times. At a time when it was most needed he did much to revive an interest in prayer and contemplation, pointed out the intimate connection between prayer and action and more than any other person was responsible for a revival of monastic life in the United States, the most remarkable revival anywhere since the Middle Ages.

'Every Christian is bound to be a person of prayer,' was Merton's deep conviction. His own life of prayer had only one aim, 'to seek and find God by love and to share that love with others'.

It is amazing to think that one Trappist (Cistercian Order) monk, vowed to a life of silence and contemplation, could exercise such a profound effect upon the development of modern spirituality.

Besides hundreds of articles for periodicals, Merton wrote

over sixty books, the underlying and unifying theme of them all being prayer. He once said, 'Whatever I may have written, I think it all can be reduced in the end to this one root truth: that God calls human persons to union with himself and with one another in Christ. And what is prayer if it is not the deepening awareness of our dependence upon God and our relationship with Him, in Christ.'

This little book is rather a concentrated presentation of Merton's teaching on prayer. I trust that the ordinary reader will not be put off reading Merton's books because of it, but rather will appreciate the riches to be gained from sharing in his exploration into the life of prayer. Many of Merton's books, like *No man is an Island* (1967), are simply written in a popular style.

Female readers are asked to be patient and understanding with Merton in his constant use of the word 'man' when he was referring to the human person. Naturally he was a male writer of his period!

I would like to thank Jacquie Galley for typing these pages for me.

Biographical Note

When Thomas Merton left New York, in December 1941, bound for Kentucky and the Cistercian Abbey of Gethsemani, the news of Pearl Harbour and America's entry into the war was ringing in his ears. Should he pursue his desire to seek God in a hidden life of prayer and contemplation, he pondered, or should he now be volunteering for the Army? He decided that at twenty-six, if he was rejected by the severe Cistercian Order (popularly known as Trappists) – as he had been by the Franciscans – he would offer himself at the recruiting office. Fortunate for us and western Christianity he was offered a trial period at the Abbey.

Thomas became Brother Louis on 19 March, 1944, when he took his first vows; and later Father Louis when he was ordained a priest in 1949. So the professor of English and author of novels and poems, who had lived a flamboyant, permissive life, like the great Augustine of Hippo, left the world behind and embraced the austerity of the Cistercian way of life. In one of his early books, *The Silent Life*, he explains that this 'austerity was not considered an end in itself but a means of putting off the "old man" corrupted by sin, and renewing the image of God, implanted by the Creator in the soul of His creature, by perfect likeness to Christ in charity'. In the monastery he experienced the love and family that had eluded him in the world.

Born of artist parents, in France in 1915, his father was from New Zealand and his mother from the United States. Thomas did not know the warmth of normal family life and could never forget how, at six years of age, his mother told him, in a formal letter, of her approaching death! Ten years later his father also died. Later he wrote of the upheavals and sadness of his early years in the internationally acclaimed *The Seven Storey Mountain* (1952).

Merton's tertiary education commenced at Cambridge University but transferred to Columbia University, and was followed by a professorship in English at St Bonaventure's University, New York. His scholarship and educational experience were put to good use in the Abbey of Gethsemani when his abbot appointed him Master of Studies for four years. This responsibility was followed by what Father Louis described as the best job in the monastery, that of Master of Novices. A post he held for ten years.

While he was Brother or Father Louis to his community, to the public he was always Thomas Merton. Although he was ever obedient to his superiors, conflicts arose over the driving need he had to write. Highly regarded and loved by his brothers in the community, for years he longed for greater solitude and in 1965 eventually obtained permission to live as a hermit in the Abbey grounds.From his hermitage poured letters to presidents, the Pope and world leaders. His life of prayer overflowed in a compelling concern for world peace, the threat of nuclear extinction and the pollution of the environment. His abbot, in return, received countless letters of complaint about the guru in his garden who was audaciously applying spiritual values to world issues!

Thomas wrote in *No Man is an Island* (the title is significant) 'Every other man is a piece of myself, for I am a part and a member of mankind. Every Christian is part of my own body, because we are members of Christ.' He really lived this belief and suffered deeply in trying to reconcile his love for the contemplative silence of the monastic life with the deep concerns thrown up by his life of prayer.

In his correspondence with the leaders of world religions, Father Louis sought for a common, spiritual unity and was particularly interested in Zen Buddhism. In 1968 he obtained permission to leave his monastery and travel to the East to address a conference in Bangkok. On the way he met the Dalai Lama and visited Sri Lanka. The story of his first real journey in twenty-seven years, which proved to be his last, is recorded in his *Asian Journal*.

He died shortly afterwards, while in Thailand, where he was accidentally electrocuted, on the twenty-seventh anniversary of his arrival at the gates of the Abbey of Gethsemani.

The personal conflict Thomas Merton experienced in 1941 on the train bound for Kentucky, between the call to a life of prayer and a life of action, was wonderfully and painfully resolved. By becoming a man of prayer and charity he became irresistibly a great man of action for, as he says himself, in the final paragraph in this little book, 'action and prayer are fused into one entity by the love of God and of our brother in Christ'.

Thomas Merton on Prayer

1   The Spiritual Life

It is impossible to think about prayer without first enquiring,
What is the Spiritual Life? It is the silence of our whole being
in compunction and adoration before God, in the habitual
realisation that he is everything and we are nothing, that he
is the centre to which all things tend, and to whom all our
actions must be directed. That our life and strength proceed
from him, that both in life and in death we depend entirely
on him.[1]

For Thomas Merton, the spiritual life consists of two
inseparable elements. First of all the human person must become
aware of the presence and goodness of God. The development
of an intimate relationship is essential and goes hand in hand
with a growing knowledge of self, the second element. No
intimate union with God is possible unless a person recognises
his or her own dignity as a child of God.

The knowledge we are speaking of, of God and self, is a loving
knowledge. 'Spiritual life is not mental life, not thought alone.
Nor is it, of course, a life of sensation, a life of feeling. Nor
does the spiritual life exclude thought and feeling. It needs
both.[1]

The spiritual life, however, is not just me and God; 'no man
is an island', but being a vital part of God's great family, with
whom I am bound by love.

13

'In order to love others with perfect charity I must be true to them, to myself and God.

'The true interests of a person are at once perfectly his own and common to the whole Kingdom of God. That is because these interests are all centred in God's designs for his soul. The destiny of each of us is intended, by the Lord, to enter into the destiny of His entire Kingdom.'[1]

2   Our Calling

Every man has a vocation to *be* someone; but he must understand clearly that in order to fulfil this vocation he can only be one person: himself.

Yet we have said that baptism gives us a sacramental character, defining our vocation in a very particular way since it tells us we must become ourselves in Christ. We must achieve our identity in him, with whom we are already sacramentally identified by water and the Holy Spirit.

What does this mean? We must be ourselves by being Christ. For a man, to be is to live. A man only lives as a man when he knows and acts according to what he loves. In this way he becomes the truth that he loves. So we 'become' Christ by knowledge and by love.

Now there is no fulfilment of man's true vocation in the order of nature. Man was made for more truth than he can see with his own unaided intelligence, and for more love than his will alone can achieve, and for a higher moral activity than human prudence ever planned.

If we know and love and act only according to the flesh, that is to say, according to the impulses of our own nature, the things we do will rapidly corrupt and destroy our whole spiritual being.

In order to be what we are meant to be, we must know Christ, and love him, and do what he did. Our destiny is in our own hands, since God has placed it there and given us his grace to do the impossible. It remains for us to take up courageously and without hesitation the work he has given us, which is the task of living our own life as Christ would live it in us.[2]

3   Made in the Image of God

According to Merton, man's capacity for perfect freedom and for pure love is what constitutes, in the human person, the image of God. 'At the very core of our essence we are constituted in God's likeness by our freedom, and the exercise of that freedom is nothing else but the exercise of disinterested love.' He writes in an unpublished work, 'The freedom that is in our nature is our ability to love something, someone besides ourselves, and for the sake, not of ourselves, but of the one we love. There is in the human will an innate tendency, an inborn capacity for disinterested love. This power to love another for his own sake is one of the things that makes us like God, because this power is the one thing in us that is free from all determination. It is a power which transcends and escapes the invevitability of self-love.'

This then is the very reason for man's existence, to realise a union with God in love. 'To say that I am made in the image of God is to say that love is the reason for my existence, for God is love.'

However, despite man's natural direction this orientation towards God has been weakened by sin. Without God's grace Divine image is not accessible. Adam's sin caused the Divine image to be disfigured and mutilated. 'He lost,' says Merton, 'his *rectitude*, and from then on it became impossible for him, without grace, to be true to himself or true to the obediential potency for union with God.'[3]

The image of God is still there in man but it is disfigured. The image of God in man – the openness to love, the capacity for total consent to God in Himself and in others – remains indestructible. But it can be buried and imprisoned under selfishness. The image of God in man is not destroyed by sin but utterly disfigured by it. To be exact, the image of God in man becomes self-contradictory when its openness closes in upon itself, when it ceases to be a capacity for love and becomes simply an appetite for domination or possession: when it ceases to give and seeks only to get . . . In monastic terms: the inclination to love, which is at the core of man's very nature as a free being, is turned in on itself as its own object and ceases to be love.'[4]

4   The Purpose of Christ

For Merton all sin is a refusal to be what we were created to be – sons of God, images of God. This failure has been rectified by the coming of the Son of God. The mystery of the Incarnation holds the key.

For although like all other mysteries it flows from the highest of all, the mystery of the Trinity, yet with regard to us the Incarnation is the most important of all because it is through Christ that we are incorporated into the life of the three Divine Persons and receive into our souls the Holy Spirit, the bond of perfection, who unites us to God with the same Love which unites the Father and the Son.[5]

Merton sees that the purpose of Christ was to restore man's union with God or re-create a new union between God and man. For the Christian, then, man's destiny for union with God can be achieved only through Christ, with Christ and in Christ; and by grace.

This is the work of the Holy Spirit to effect this new creation or to regenerate a new man in Christ.

5   Union with Christ

A 'new being' is brought into existence. I become a 'new man', and this 'new man' spiritually and mystically one identity, is at once Christ and myself . . . . This spiritual union of my being with Christ in one 'new man' is the work of the Holy Spirit, the Spirit of Love, the Spirit of Christ.

. . . The union of my soul with God in Christ is not of this ontological or inseparable character. It is, on the contrary, an accidental union; yet it is more than just a moral union or an agreement of hearts. The union of the Christian with Christ . . . is a mystical union in which Christ Himself becomes the source and principle of divine life in me. Christ Himself, . . . 'breathes' in me divinely in giving me His Spirit.[6]

The new person, possessed by the Spirit, must try to penetrate the inner meaning of his life in Christ. The Holy Spirit . . . not only makes us understand something of God's love as it is manifested to us in Christ, but He also makes us live by that love and experience its action in our hearts. When we do so, the Spirit lets us know that this life and action are the life and action of Christ in us. And so the charity that is poured forth in our hearts by the Holy Spirit, brings us into an intimate, experiential communion with Christ.[2]

6   A Life of Love

The calling then is to a life of love for . . . this love is the very root of our being. Therefore what we are called to do is to live as habitually and constantly as possible with great simplicity on this level of love which proceeds from the depths of our own being where Christ reigns and loves. This is a dimension of life which no one can take away unless we close the door ourselves and no one can bring it in unless we open the door to Christ, opening our hearts to Christ and dwelling there.[7]

Accepting God's love in faith implies the need to share both that love and that faith. To further his or her union with God in faith and love must be the ultimate reason for the existence of each Christian.

If Christians living in the world are to live as true members of Christ and radiate the divine influence among the people with whom they are in contact, they will be obliged to develop rich interior lives of union with God, and this union will have to be deep enough to weather the demands of hard work and constant contact with things that would defile a weaker spirit.[8]

The calling or vocation of man is clear; God's intentions and plan for the human person seems evident, but there has to be a response. There has to be a 'turning towards' God.

The Spirit, however, does not accomplish His work in man if man remains completely passive and inert. If man is to enter fully into the mystery of this supernatural union in Christ, he must respond to God's gift of grace and consent to live as a son of God.

'If we would live like sons of God, we must reproduce in our own lives the life and the charity of His only begotten son.'[2]

'It is the easiest thing in the world to possess this life . . . ; all you have to do is believe and love.'[2]

7   God Within

The purpose of life then is to grow continuously, through the Holy Spirit, in union with the risen Christ towards the complete

18

maturity and perfection which is Christ living in the human person and uniting people to one another.

As Merton points out in *No Man is an Island:* 'Each one of us becomes completely himself when, in the Spirit of God, he is transformed in Christ.'

A Christian, then, in Merton's view, is searching for God only when he is aware both of God and of others in God in his life and only when he realises through love that he has been transformed in Christ by God. The problem today, Merton believed, is that many Christians fail to realise this truth. They 'too often fail to realise that the infinite God is dwelling within them, so that He is in them and they are in Him. They remain unaware of the presence of the infinite source of being right in the midst of the world and of men.' He then goes on to say: 'What is required of Christians is that they develop a completely modern and contemporary consciousness in which their experience as men of our century is integrated with their experience as children of God redeemed by Christ.[9]

8   Recollection

Recollection is a change of spiritual focus and an attuning of our whole soul to what is beyond and above ourselves. Spiritual things are simple, so recollection is a simplification of our state of mind and spiritual activity. It gives us the kind of peace and vision which comes from directing all our love to God Himself. And it is by peace, interior silence and tranquillity that recollection can be known.

Merton says: 'the spirit that is recollected is quiet and detached, at least in its depths. It is undisturbed because the passions are momentarily at rest. At most, they are allowed to trouble only the surface of the recollected soul'.[2]

Recollection is not a form of concentration, nor is it a denial or shutting out of exterior things.

> 'Recollection should be seen not as an absence, but as a presence. It makes us present to ourselves; it makes us present to whatever reality is most significant in the moment of time in which we are living. And it makes us present to God and brings his presence to us.'[2]

Recollection makes us present to ourselves by making us live the present moment, not some vague future possibility or some past dead happening. Recollection helps us to make the present real. 'The present is our right place, and we can lay hands on whatever it offers us. Recollection is the only thing that can give us the power to do so.'[2]

Recollection also makes us present to God, and to ourselves in Him. It is true that we are always present to God who sees all and keeps all things in existence but we are more present to Him when we are aware of His nearness to us. 'For then the presence is conscious and mutual; it is the presence of a person to a person. And it is only when we are thus present to Him that we truly discover ourselves as we really are.'[2]

9   Prayer – living the Union

Contemplative prayer, for Merton, is more to do with the orientation of one's prayer life than the narrow restricted meaning usually attached to it. Because everyone has the need to listen to God in silence, grow in faith and love and try to live in an atmosphere of prayer; the contemplative orientation lies essentially in surrendering to God.

'Prayer then means yearning for the simple presence of God, for a personal understanding of his word, for knowledge of his will and for a capacity to hear and obey him.'[10] It is thus something much more than uttering petitions for good things external to our deepest concerns, or repetitious praise.

Those words were distilled from years of prayerful searching. Merton's early steps in prayer are recorded in his *The Seven Storey Mountain*.

'And now I think for the first time in my whole life I really began to pray – praying not with my lips and with my intellect and my imagination, but praying out of the very roots of my life and of my being, and praying to the God I had never known, to reach down towards me out of His darkness and to help me to get free of the thousand terrible things that held my will in their slavery.'

Prayer is inspired by God in the depth of our own nothingness. It is the movement of trust, of gratitude, of adoration, or of sorrow that places us before God, seeing both Him and ourselves in the light of His infinite truth, and moves us to ask Him for the mercy, the spiritual strength, the material help that we all need. The man whose prayer is so pure that he never asks God for anything, does not know who God is, and does not know who he is himself: for he does not know his own need of God.

All true prayer somehow confesses our absolute dependence on the Lord of life and death. It is, therefore, a deep and vital contact with Him whom we know not only as Lord but as Father. It is when we pray truly that we really are. Our being is brought to a high perfection by this, which is one of its most perfect activities. When we cease to pray, we tend to fall back into nothingness. True, we continue to exist. But since the main reason for our existence is the knowledge and love of God, when our conscious contact with Him is severed we sleep or we die.[2]

10 Meditation

Merton found the term 'mental prayer' misleading for we rarely pray with the 'mind' alone. Monastic meditation, prayer, contemplation and reading involve the whole man, and proceed from the 'centre' of man's being, his 'heart' renewed in the Holy Spirit, totally submissive to the grace of Christ. Monastic prayer begins with a 'return to the heart', finding one's deepest centre, awakening the profound depths of our being in the presence of God who is the source of our being and our life.[10]

Although he acknowledged the importance of the intellect and the will in achieving a loving spiritual contact with God in Christ, Merton constantly emphasises that the *whole* person meditates.

In meditative prayer, one thinks and speaks not only with one's mind and lips, but in a certain sense with one's whole being. Prayer is then not just a formula of words, or a series of desires springing up in the heart – it is the orientation of our whole body, mind and spirit to God in silence, attention and adoration. All good meditative prayer is a conversion of our entire self to God.[1]

In meditation we do not seek to know *about* God as though he were an object like other objects which submit to our scrutiny and can be expressed in clear scientific ideas. We seek to know God Himself, the infinite God, who has no boundaries and our mind cannot set limits to Him or to His love. His presence is then 'grasped' in the general awareness of loving faith, it is 'realised' without being scientifically and precisely known. The aim then of meditation is to come to know God through the realisation that our very being is penetrated with his knowledge and love for us.[11]

11   Prayer of the Heart

In another work, *Monastic Peace*, Merton goes on to show that it is because prayer embraces a person's whole being that it is possible for men to live consciously in an atmosphere of prayer.

Meditation is really a meeting with someone whom we already possess, a gradual realisation of our own wretchedness and nothingness in the presence of God. In 'prayer of the heart', as Merton preferred to call meditation, we are confronted by the deepest reality of our relationship with God. ' "Meditation" or "prayer of the heart" is the active effort we make to keep our hearts open so that we may be enlightened by him and filled with his realisation of our true relation to him.'[10]

Prayer of the heart is the active effort we make to keep our hearts open and discover our spiritual poverty and need for God. To come to realise that we have 'no other reason for being, except to be loved by him as Creator and Redeemer, and to love him in return.'[10]

12   In Compunction and Dread

So to meditation must be brought two fundamental attitudes – *compunction* and *dread*. Merton sees this as vital and liberating. The inward movement of compunction is not so much a matter of hiding ourselves, as a liberation of ourselves, which takes place in the depths of our being, and lets us out of ourselves from the inside. This liberation from concentration on ourself is the beginning of a conversion, a *metanoia*, a real inner transformation.[12]

The experience of 'dread', 'nothingness' and 'night' in the

heart of man is then the awareness of infidelity to the truth of our life. More, it is an awareness of infidelity as unrepented and without grace as unrepentable. It is the deep, confused, metaphysical awareness of a basic antagonism between the self and God caused by estrangement from him by perverse attachment to a 'self' which is mysterious and illusory.[10]

13   Simple Affective Prayer

In his book, *What Are These Wounds*, Merton speaks of the simplicity of affective prayer for those who have progressed in their life of prayer and says:

> It is clear that those who have progressed a certain distance in the interior life not only do not need to make systematic meditations, but rather profit by abandoning them in favour of a simple and peaceful affective prayer, without fuss, without voice, without much speech, and with no more than one or two favourite ideas or mysteries, to which they return in a more or less general and indistinct manner each time they pray.

However, it is contemplation which is the fruit of an earnest life of prayer. 'Contemplation', he says, 'is the fullness of the Christian vocation, the full flowing of baptismal grace of the Christ-life in our souls.'[13]

14 Contemplation

Merton has described Contemplation in the following words:

> Contemplation is the highest expression of man's intellectual
> and spiritual life . . . It is a vivid realisation of the fact that
> life and being in us proceed from an invisible, transcendent
> and infinitely abundant Source. Contemplation is, above all,
> awareness of the reality of that Source. It *knows* the Source,
> obscurely, inexplicably, but with a certitude that goes beyond
> reason and simple faith.
>
> In other words, then, contemplation reaches out to the
> knowledge and even to the experience of the transcendent and
> inexpressible God . . . Hence contemplation is a sudden gift
> of awareness, an awakening to the Real within all that is real.
> A vivid awareness of infinite Being at the roots of our own
> limited being. An awareness of our contingent reality as
> received, as a present from God, as a free gift of love.
>
> It is the religious apprehension of God, through my life in
> God, or through 'sonship'. . . . And so the contemplation of
> which I speak is a religious and transcendent gift . . . It is
> the gift of God Who, in His mercy, completes the hidden and
> mysterious work of creation in us by enlightening our minds
> and hearts, by awakening in us the awareness that we are
> words spoken in His One Word, and that Creating Spirit . . .
> dwells in us and we in Him. That we are 'in Christ' and that
> Christ lives in us. That the natural life in us has been
> completed, elevated, transformed and fulfilled in Christ by
> the Holy Spirit. Contemplation is the awareness and
> realisation, even in some sense *experience*, of what each
> Christian obscurely believes: 'It is now no longer I that live
> but Christ lives in me.'[6]

The 'knowing' spoken of is a recognition of God as Love. 'We do not see God in contemplation – we know Him by love: for He is pure love and when we taste the experience of loving God for His own sake alone, we know by experience who and what He is.'[14]

15 Contemplation is for All

Man recognises the fact that God is Love and so loves Him for His own sake. Merton frequently notes that while a person may work for and desire this gift, it remains a gift. 'If anyone should ask, "Who may desire this gift and pray for it?" The answer is obvious: everybody.'[14]

'Contemplation, by which we know and love God as He is in Himself, apprehending Him in a deep and vital experience which is beyond the reach of any natural understanding, is the reason for our creation by God.'[6] For we are called to be sons and daughters of God and contemplation is essentially an experience of our divine sonship. It is an experiential recognition, a 'taste', an interior awakening, an intimate and personal appreciation of the truth that God loves us not only as our Creator but as our Father. More, that He is actually present to us as our 'Father', that is, as the source of our supernatural life, our charity.[15]

Contemplation does not cut us off from life. It is not a separate 'holy' department of the praying Christian's life. True contemplation is inseparable from life and from the dynamism of life – which includes work, creation, production, fruitfulness and above all love. Contemplation is not to be thought of as a separate department of life, cut off from all man's other interests and superseding them. It is the very fulness of a fully integrated life. It is the crown of life and of all life's activities.[16]

16   Action and Contemplation

For Merton a person's whole life can become a prayer. By living as habitually as possible on this level of union and love, daily life and its work can further and deepen our spiritual life.

'Work can help us to pray and be recollected if we work properly . . . Work brings peace to the soul that has a semblance of order and spiritual understanding. It helps the soul to focus upon its spiritual aims and to achieve them.[2]

Action and prayer for the true Christian are inseparable. 'Far from being essentially opposed to each other, interior contemplation and external activity are two aspects of the same love of God.'[6]

Action and contemplation now grow together into one life and one unity. They become two aspects of the same thing. Action is charity looking outward to other men, and contemplation is charity drawn inward to its own divine source. Action is the stream, and contemplation is the spring. The spring remains more important than the stream, for the only thing that really matters is for love to spring up inexhaustibly from the infinite abyss of Christ and of God.[2]

If we pray 'in the Spirit' we are certainly not running away from life, negating visible reality in order to 'see God'. For 'the Spirit of the Lord has filled the whole earth.' Prayer does not blind us to the world, but it transforms our vision of the world, and makes us see it, all men, and all the history of mankind, in the light of God. To pray 'in spirit and in truth' enables us to enter into contact with that infinite love, that inscrutable freedom which is at work behind the complexities and the intricacies of human existence. This does not mean fabricating for ourselves pious rationalisations to explain everything that happens. It involves no surreptitious manipulation of the hard truths of life.

Meditation does not necessarily give us a privileged insight into the meaning of isolated historical events. These can remain for the Christian as much of an agonising mystery as they do for anyone else. But for us the mystery contains, within its own darkness and its own silences, a presence and a meaning which we apprehend without fully understanding them. And by this spiritual contact, this act of faith, we are ourselves properly situated in the events around us, even though we may not quite see where they are going.[11]

Action and contemplation are fused into one entity by the love of God and of our brother in Christ. But the trouble is that if prayer is not itself deep, powerful and pure and filled at all times with the spirit of contemplation, Christian action can never really reach this high level.

The most important need in the Christian world today is this inner truth nourished by the Spirit of contemplation: the praise and love of God, the longing for the coming of Christ, the thirst for the manifestation of God's glory, his truth, his justice, his Kingdom in the world. These are all characteristically 'contemplative' and eschatological aspirations of the Christian heart, and they are the very essence of prayer.[11]

Sources

1. *Thoughts in Solitude* (Image Books, 1968).
2. *No Man is an Island* (Image Books, 1967).
3. *The Spirit of Simplicity* (Abbey of Gethsemani, 1948).
4. *The Monastic Theology of Aelred of Rievaulx* (Intro. by Merton: Cistercian Publications, 1969).
5. *The Ascent to Truth* (Harcourt, Brace, 1951).
6. *New Seeds of Contemplation* (New Directions, 1961).
7. A Conference on Prayer (India) unpublished.
8. *The White Peeble* (*Sign* July 1950.)
9. *Faith and Violence* (Notre Dame Press, 1968).
10. The Climate of Monastic Prayer (*C.O.C.R.* (27) 1965).
11. *Contemplative Prayer* (Herder and Herder, 1969).
12. *Seasons of Celebration* (Farrer, Strauss & Giroux, 1964).
13. *Poetry or Contemplation* (*Commonweal* (69) 1958).
14. *What is Contemplation?* (Burns & Oates 1950).
15. The Psalms and Contemplation (*Orate Frates* (24) 1950).
16. *A Thomas Merton Reader* (Harcourt, Brace 1962).